Get the
Dope on Dope
First Response Guide
to Street Drugs
Volume One
3rd Edition
Sixth Printing

NOTE:

The symptoms of drug use can vary from person to person and, in particular when someone is under the complex influence of two or more drugs.

Use extreme caution when using these charts. They are intended **only** as a guide.

---

www.dopeondope.com

ON-SITE STREET & CLUB DRUG AWARENESS TRAINING NOW AVAILABLE!

Leading drug expert and award-winning author Steve Walton now offers intensive on-site drug training programs for a wide variety of groups including:

- Law enforcement agencies & security personnel
- Emergency medical services professionals
- Parent, school & community action program
- Hospitals, Addiction Clinics and other medical outlets
- Corporations, human resources professionals…

And any individual or group who has need for drug awareness in the course of their work, the protection of their families or the control of their organizational environment.

Classes are offered on a customized basis at a time and location of your choosing and at various pre-determined locations throughout North America.

For full details on curriculum, pricing and scheduling please contact:

U.S. LOCATIONS
Scott Buhrmaster, Chicago Office
Phone: (773) 481-4964 • Fax: (773) 913-6205
scott@publishingpromo.com

CANADIAN LOCATIONS
Heather Walton, Calgary Office
Phone: (403) 255-5605 • Fax: (403) 258-3696
dopeondope@shaw.ca

Toll-Free in U.S. and Canada
(877) 255-1166

STREET & CLUB DRUG AWARENESS TRAINING TOPICS INCLUDE:

- Drug recognition instruction for today's most popular and dangerous street and club drugs
- Current North American drug trends
- Methods and indicators of use
- Safety issues for first responders, parents, teachers and any others intervening in a drug use situation
- Interpretation of current drug lingo
- Information of drugs and drug activities specific to your area
- And much, much more!

Steve Walton's drug training has been hailed as the best program available in North America.

Full and complete satisfaction is assured.

Call for full details!

U.S. LOCATIONS
Scott Buhrmaster, Chicago Office
Phone: (773) 481-4964 • Fax: (773) 913 6205
scott@publishingpromo.com

CANADIAN LOCATIONS
Heather Walton, Calgary Office
Phone: (403) 255-5605 • Fax: (403) 258-3696
dopeondope@shaw.ca

Toll-Free in U.S. and Canada
(877) 255-1166

Get the Dope on Dope:
First Response Guide to Street Drugs
Volume One
3rd Edition
Sixth Printing

Published by
Burnand Holding Co. Ltd.
420 52 Ave. S.W.
Calgary, Alberta, Canada T2V 0A9

ISBN 0-9689269-0-8

Printed in Canada

Index

Introduction

This guide is intended to lead people to a better understanding of the true perils of street drugs. In providing informed, up to date and practical insight into the effects of some of the most common street drugs in use today, it is hoped that this understanding will be achieved. This guide was also developed to answer some pertinent questions about how the most common street drugs react according to first-hand accounts. To that end, this guide deals with the drugs most often encountered on the street.

In the following pages, readers will discover a phenomenon, which is referred to as the *Rhomberg Internal Clock.* For clarification purposes, this clock can be an indicator of drug use. It was not developed by the author of this book, only adapted to further assist readers in their understanding of street drugs. When applying this test, simply have the subject of the test close their eyes and estimate when they believe 30 seconds have expired. The subject will of course be timed and depending on the drug consumed, the test subject will have difficulty accurately estimating the 30-second time span. The test should be used in conjunction with other observations of the subject's physiology and behaviour in order to reach a legitimate conclusion. It should be remembered that in many instances, there might well be a combination of drugs in use simultaneously, which could give a different spin on the individual's symptoms and responses (see "Potentiation" in the glossary).

Cocaine $C_{17}H_{21}NO_4$

Key Facts

What is it?	Central Nervous System Stimulant
Physiological Responses	Quick surge of energy for a short period of time
	Causes confusion and disorganized thinking pattern
	Impairs judgment
	Talkative
	Excited
	Irrational
	The short term physiological effects of cocaine include constricted blood vessels; increased temperature, heart rate, and blood pressure. Large amounts (several hundred milligrams or more) intensify the user's high, but may also lead to bizarre, erratic, and violent behaviour. These users may experience tremors, vertigo, muscle twitches, paranoia, or, with repeated doses, a toxic reaction closely resembling Amphetamine poisoning. Some users of Cocaine report feelings of restlessness, irritability, and anxiety. In rare instances, sudden death can occur on the first use of Cocaine or unexpectedly thereafter. Cocaine-related deaths are often a result of cardiac arrest or seizures followed by respiratory arrest.
Eye Characteristics	Dilated pupil, pupil response to light stimulus is slow
Rhomberg Internal Clock	Fast
How long do the effects last?	Generically, the Cocaine high is intense, but short in duration
	45 minutes for powdered Cocaine

	20 minutes for base Cocaine
Onset of Action	3 – 5 seconds if smoked (base Cocaine)
	15 minute onset of action if Cocaine Hydrochloride is inhaled (snorted)
	15 – 30 second onset of action if the Cocaine Hydrochloride is injected intravenously
Effects of Use	Euphoric, energetic, talkative, and mentally alert, especially to the sensations of sight, sound, and touch. It can also temporarily decrease the need for food and sleep. Some users find that the drug helps them to perform simple physical and intellectual tasks more quickly, while others can experience the opposite effect.
How is it Taken?	Inhaled (snorted)
	Injected
	Smoked – base Cocaine
Negative Effects of Use	Severe "crash" once high is complete
	Disturbances in heart rhythm
	Heart attacks
	Respiratory failure
	Strokes
	Seizure
	Headaches
	Abdominal pain and nausea. Cocaine use has been linked to many types of heart disease. Cocaine has been found to trigger chaotic heart rhythms, called ventricular fibrillation; accelerated heartbeat and breathing; and increase in blood pressure and body temperature. Physical symptoms may include chest pain, nausea, blurred vision, fever, muscle spasms, convulsions and coma.

Different routes of Cocaine administration can produce different adverse effects. Regularly snorting cocaine, for example, can lead to loss of sense of smell, nosebleeds, problems with swallowing, hoarseness, and an overall irritation of the nasal septum, which can lead to a chronically inflamed, runny nose. Ingested Cocaine can cause severe bowel gangrene, due to reduced blood flow. Persons who inject cocaine have puncture marks and "tracks" most commonly under their forearms. Intravenous Cocaine users may also experience an allergic reaction, either to the drug, or to some additive in street Cocaine, which can result, in severe cases, in death. Because Cocaine has a tendency to decrease food intake, many chronic Cocaine users lose their appetites and can experience significant weight loss and malnourishment.

Other Information Related to Cocaine

Possibility of Physical Addiction	Cocaine Hydrochloride is physically addictive and can cause a psychological dependence
	Physically addicted to Cocaine Hydrochloride within 6 to 10 months
	Physically addicted to base or rock Cocaine within 30 days
Physical Characteristics of Substance	White powder
	Chunks which are a light yellow in appearance

Odours Associated to Substance	Chemical smell when smoked (base Cocaine)
	Kerosene - like smell (Cocaine Hydrochloride)
Drug Paraphernalia	Needles, pipes, razor blades, small mirrors
Dosage	When inhaled, 10 to 25 milligrams per nostril per dose
Safety Issues for Medical Personnel	Violence, Unpredictable behaviour, Paranoia
Associated Drugs	Methamphetamine, Ecstasy
Street Pricing	$60-$100 per gram (Cocaine Hydrochloride)
	$40-$50 per 1/4 gram "rock" (base Cocaine)
Common Street Names	Blow
	Coke
	White
	Up
	Hard (base cocaine)
	Soft (cocaine hydrochloride)
Other Dangers	Poor needle habits
	Use of other stimulants

Cocaine is a powerful Central Nervous System Stimulant, which is derived from the leaves of the Coca plant (Erythroxylon). This plant is indigenous to South America and is grown in Peru, Bolivia, and Columbia. Eighty percent of the Coca plants in the world come from Peru. Eighty percent of the Cocaine extraction laboratories in the world are in Colombia.

The two most popular forms of this drug are:

- Cocaine Hydrochloride (powder)
- Cocaine base (crack or rock)

Cocaine Hydrochloride is water-soluble and can be inhaled, ingested, or injected. Cocaine base has been converted via chemical reaction from the Hydrochloride form and once the conversion process is complete is no longer soluble in water and therefore is most often smoked.

Cocaine

There are several public safety issues, which surround the manufacturing, distribution, and consumption of this drug regardless of what form it takes. Firstly, at the consumer level, Cocaine is a very addictive substance; it is also very expensive ($80.00 to $100.00 per gram for the powder, $100.00 to $150.00 per gram for the base). The cycle of abuse for consumers of the powder is approximately 6 months. This means that after 6 months of casual use, the consumer develops a physical addiction. This cycle becomes shortened if they are using it more often than on a casual basis. The cycle of abuse for the base form is considerably less. In some cases this cycle can be 30 days however, in more extreme cases the cycle could be 1 week. The base form of the drug is considerably more addictive than the Hydrochloride form. This is a very dangerous combination (expense and addiction) as the resulting addicts have a difficult time affording their new habit and turn to various forms of street crime to finance their Cocaine purchases. It then becomes obvious where the public safety issue develops. The Cocaine "high" is also problematic since it lasts for a relatively short period of time. In the case of Cocaine Hydrochloride, generically the high would last for approximately 1 hour. When Cocaine addicts have resorted to intravenous use of the drug, it is not uncommon for them to inject 18 to 20 times every 24 hours. Base Cocaine provides the consumer with an overwhelming state of intoxication however, generically this high lasts for approximately 20 minutes.

Due to the profitability of the trafficking of this drug, organized crime is heavily involved in it. With the involvement of both organized and not so organized groups the propensity for street violence due to the on-going competition is magnified and so is the danger to the public at large.

There is also a more global issue with respect to addiction and the public health care system. Individuals who are addicted to cocaine usually resort to injection of the hydrochloride form or smoking the base form. In any case, the addiction and the problems caused by it are compounded by other health care situations that street drug addicts are historically afflicted with. This places an additional burden on an already over-worked health care system, which for the most part is funded by the public.

In summary, cocaine by its nature is a dangerous street drug. Whether you are a police officer sworn to protect the public, or whether you are a front line Health Care giver devoted to providing professional health care to the public or whether you are the public going about your daily business, the dangers of this street drug can reach out and touch you at a moment's notice.

NOTES

Ecstasy

Methylenedioxymethamphetamine $C_{11}H_{15}NO_2$

Key Facts

What is it?	Central Nervous System Stimulant
	Hallucinogenic Amphetamine
Physiological Responses	Increased blood pressure
	Jaw clenching
	Teeth grinding
	Increased pulse rate
	Increased body temperature
	Nausea
	Anxiety
	Paranoid thoughts (for example; fear of persecution or feelings of superiority)
	Sweating
	Dehydration
	Sensations of floating
	Irrational behaviour
	Blurred vision
	Convulsions
	Difficulty Concentrating (especially the day after taking the drug known as the "Ecstasy Hangover Syndrome")
Eye Characteristics	Pupils are dilated, pupil response to light is slow
Rhomberg Internal Clock	Fast
How long do the effects last?	Most effects last up to 6 hours, but some may persist for up to 60 hours
Onset of Action	Within 45 minutes of consumption
Effects of Use	Feelings of energy
	Appetite suppressed

	Hallucinations
	Strong feelings of well being
	Increased confidence
	Feelings of closeness with other people
	Colours are brighter
	Music sounds better
	Sense of smell is affected to the point where users will sniff products like mentholated rub from filter masks or carry and use nasal inhalers.
	Sense of touch is heightened - users of the drug will compulsively touch one another and will even carry stuffed toys, which are also compulsively touched
How is it Taken?	Taken orally in tablet form
	Original form is white powder that can be diluted in water and sprayed in eyes or on skin. It can also be injected and snorted
Negative Effects of Use	Insomnia
	Depression
	Muscle aches
	Impacts metabolic rates (increase)
	Brain damage
	Heart damage due to high, sustained heart rates
	Liver damage
	Very high blood pressure
	Fast heartbeat
	Very high body temperature
	Death

Ecstasy

Other Information Related to Ecstasy

Possibility of Physical Addiction	Use is likely to cause psychological dependence, however, recent studies demonstrate a correlation between use and addiction
Physical Characteristics of Substance	In original state it is found in a white powder form. Can be made into tablets of varying sizes and colours
Odours Associated to Substance	None
Drug Paraphernalia	Baby Pacifiers Lollypops Toothbrushes Feather Necklaces Stuffed Animals Spray Bottles Water Bottles
Dosage	The normal street dose is 80 to 160 milligrams "Stacking" - when the drug is taken at regular intervals. eg. Consumers take 100 mg at 1700 hrs, another 100 mg at 2100 hrs – this leads to long lasting stimulation and intoxication.
Safety Issues for Medical Personnel	Avoid being sprayed by "water" in bottles Hostile to Persons in Authority – doctors, nurses, paramedics, police officers when hallucinating
Associated Drugs	Ketamine L.S.D. Methamphetamine G.H.B.

Street Pricing	$10 to $25 per 50 mg dose (Year 2000)
Common Street Names	E
	X
	EVA
	LOVE DRUG
	DANCE DRUG
	EVERYTHING DRUG
	XTC
	E's
	ECKIES
	ADAM
	HUG DRUG
	BLUEBERRY*
	STRAWBERRY*
	BANANA*
	*Names coincide with the colour of the tablet or the powder
Other Dangers	Manipulating purity of Ecstasy by cutting it with LSD, PMA (Paramethoxyamphetamine) and DXM (Dextromethorphan)

ECSTASY: Is it all the rave?

Ecstasy has become very popular in a relatively short period of time. Although it was originally synthesized many years ago in the early 1900's, it started to develop a true following as an illegal street drug in the late 1980's. The consumer age range for this drug has evolved rapidly over the last 3 years and is inclusive from 12 to 25 years. The age group over 25 years has also

Ecstasy

discovered the drug; this demographic group has disposable income and is searching for a stimulant drug of choice other than Cocaine.

As mentioned, this drug is classified as an Hallucinogenic Amphetamine, which is usually sold as small tablets that come in a variety of colours and sizes. The colour and size is limited only to the capabilities of the laboratory producing it and to the imagination of the producers. It has also been found in gelatine capsules.

The original form of this drug is a white powder, prior to tabletting. In its powder form it can be inhaled through the nose, injected, or absorbed (it is water soluble). A major issue surrounding Ecstasy is the purity level of the drug. People need to understand that in and of itself, M.D.M.A. presents very real adverse health issues. A disturbing trend, which has been recently identified, is the presence of other dangerous substances in conjunction with, or in place of M.D.M.A. These other substances include but are not limited to:

- P.M.A. (paramethoxyamphetamine) a very powerful, extremely toxic Amphetamine
- D.X.M. (dextromethorphan) a cough suppressant commonly seen in medications. This substance has a perspiration suppression capability

The presence of the above substances compounds the health risks to consumers.

The drug is illegally produced in clandestine laboratories. Historically, these labs were found mostly in Europe however, it is becoming more common to see the lab sites on our continent. For many years the drug has arrived in North America from the Netherlands however, as the synthesis for the drug becomes more common knowledge and the "recipes" become simpler and more available, the drug will be produced right here on our continent in clandestine laboratories.

Consumers of this drug will find that the drug has an impact on the metabolic rates and can cause brain damage through stroke and inter-cranial pressure. The drug can also cause heart damage due to high, sustained heart rates, and can cause liver damage. Due to the fact that this drug causes the body temperature to increase, users can suffer serious and fatal complications from this phenomenon. What must be remembered is that people have died and will continue to die as a result of having consumed ecstasy.

One issue that continues to arise in emergency rooms is that the symptoms suffered from Ecstasy often mimic those associated with Meningitis.

As outlined in the key facts reference chart,(Page 12) there are problems with both addiction and dependence when dealing with this drug. Another major issue is the tolerance that is developed with the chronic use of this drug. Humans have a tendency to tolerate M.D.M.A. quite rapidly and what that means is the more often you take the drug the more you have to take to feel the effects. This is problematic and can lead to a very expensive habit that some consumers have difficulty affording.

Ecstasy can produce severe hallucinations, people who have taken high doses sometimes behave irrationally when they are experiencing these hallucinations and can be dangerous to themselves or others.

This drug affects the way in which we receive and transmit Seratonin. Seratonin is an important neurotransmitter that regulates our moods, assists us in our learning processes and contributes to memory development, storage, and retrieval. Unfortunately, for the consumers of this drug, recent studies indicate that M.D.M.A. adversely effects the production, transmission, and reception of Seratonin.

Much of the paraphernalia associated to the use of this drug is utilized as a type of safety equipment. The use of pacifiers and lollipops is preventative in nature, as the drug causes users to clench their jaws, grind their teeth and bite the inside of their mouth. Placing an object in the mouth prevents injury from these symptoms.

G.H.B.

(Gamma-hydroxybutyrate) $C_4H_8O_3$

Key Facts

What is it?	Central Nervous System Depressant
Physiological Responses	Lowered heart rate
	Lowered respiration
	Loss of gag reflex
Eye Characteristics	Pupil size is near normal, pupil response to light is slow
Rhomberg Internal Clock	Slow
How long do the effects last?	Last from 8 – 12 hours
Onset of Action	Approximately 15 minutes
Effects of Use	Intoxication
	Increased energy
	Happiness
	Talking
	Desire to socialize
	Feeling affectionate and playful
	Mild lack of inhibition
	Sensuality and sexual experience enhanced
	Muscle relaxation,
How is it Taken?	A liquid that is taken orally and can be mixed with alcohol
Negative Effects of Use	Loss of coordination due to loss of muscle tone
	Nausea
	Difficulty concentrating
	Death from Overdose

Other Information Related to G.H.B.

Possibility of Physical Addiction	This substance can cause physical addiction
Physical Characteristics of Substance	Liquid Wax like solid form Also found in powder form
Odours Associated to Substance	Mild chemical smell if good quality or a strong chemical smell if poor quality
Drug Paraphernalia	Water bottles, sports drink bottles, purse-size hair spray containers, mouthwash bottles, vitamin or other pill containers, eyedroppers, liquid candy containers.
Dosage	Taken in small amounts referred to as "capfuls" 1.5 – 2.5grams
Safety Issues for Medical Personnel	This drug causes severe intoxication and can lead to irrational behaviour
Associated Drugs	Ecstasy, Ketamine, LSD
Street Pricing	$5 to $20 per dose
Common Street Names	G Gross Bodily Harm Easy Lay Cherry Meth Everclear
Other Dangers	C.N.S. Depressant which slows the heart rate to dangerously low levels Possibility of Coma No chemical antidote

G.H.B. is a highly addictive substance that has become popular as a "club drug". It is easily made in kitchen laboratories and is also popular as a clandestine chemical for sexual predators.

It has a salty taste that many people hide in alcoholic drinks like Margaritas, Long Island Iced Tea. GHB is also hidden in sports drinks.

NOTES

G.H.B.

Heroin

(Diacetylmorphine) $C_{21}H_{23}NO_5$

Key Facts

What is it?	Central Nervous System Depressant
Physiological Responses	Drowsiness
	Nausea
	Vomiting
	Respiratory depression
	Heart rate reduced
	Slowed and slurred speech
	Slow gait
	Constipation
Eye Characteristics	Constricted pupils, watery eyes, droopy eyelids
Rhomberg Internal Clock	Slow
How long do the effects last?	Eight hours
Onset of Action	Rapid onset of action (several seconds to several minutes depending on method of use)
Effects of Use	Initially produces a strong feeling of euphoria, followed by:
	Widening of the blood vessels, causes a warm feeling
	Relaxed detachment from pain (narcotic analgesic)
How is it Taken?	Normally injected, however, it can also be smoked, and inhaled (snorted)
Negative Effects of Use	H.I.V. infection from injection
	Slow, irregular heart rate
	Irregular blood pressure

Convulsions (part of withdrawal
syndrome)

Tolerance and addiction

Death from overdose

Other Information Related to Heroin

Possibility of Physical Addiction	According to California studies done in 1997, there is a 97% addiction rate after one-time use.
Physical Characteristics of Substance	Original state is a powder. The colour ranges from brown to white
Odours Associated to Substance	Chemical smell when burned
Drug Paraphernalia	Syringes, spoons with bent handles, filter tips from cigarettes
Dosage	Average dose is a 1/4 of 1 point (a point is 1/10th of a gram) this dose level sustains the heroin habit. Maximum dose is 1 point Usually packaged in caps and bundles (gel caps, condoms)
Safety Issues for Medical Personnel	Infectious diseases from consumers through the use of needles which include HIV & Hepatitis
Associated Drugs	Morphine, methadone
Street Pricing	1 point = $40.00 to $60.00 1 gram = $300.00 to $400.00 1 ounce = up to $7,000.00
Common Street Names	Down Smack Horse H

Heroin

Other Dangers	Once tolerance is developed, positive pleasure from the drug is replaced by relief at simply taking the drug to maintain "normality"

Heroin; the rest of the story

What is it?

Heroin is converted Morphine

Morphine is derived from Opium

Opium is derived from the Opium poppy "Papaver Somniferum"

How is it made?

13 kgs of raw Opium= 1 kg of Morphine base

1 kg of morphine base= 1 kg of 100% pure Heroin

One acre of poppies produces 6-8 kgs of raw Opium

Heroin is approximately 3 times more powerful than Morphine

Another form of Heroin known as "black tar" is available in the Western United States.

Black tar Heroin is produced in Mexico and its purity ranges from 20% to 50%

There is a five step process which converts Morphine to Heroin

Heroin by the numbers:

Heroin number 1: a tan to brown powder, which is actually not Heroin but crude Morphine base extracted from raw Opium

Heroin number 2: a white to grey powder, which is a transitional step in the conversion of Heroin from Morphine base. Heroin number 2 is the foundation for the next two types of Heroin

Heroin number 3: a tan to grey granular powder also known as "Smoking Heroin". This form of Heroin is usually 40% pure, and it is common to hear "Chasing the Dragon" in conjunction with the use of Heroin number 3

Heroin number 4: a white to creamy yellow powder, usually 95% pure, high degree of solubility in water

The average purity of Heroin is 78%

What is the history of Heroin?

Heroin was first synthesized by an English scientist (C. R. Wright) in 1874

The Bayer Company of Germany first produced the drug commercially in 1898.

At that time, it was widely advertised as the new "miracle drug" and marketed as a cure for Opium and Morphine addiction.

During this time, the drug manufacturers and the medical profession did not understand the nature of the drug.

Heroin

As a result of this ignorance, the drug was widely prescribed and administered.

Subsequently, Heroin, due to its nature, replaced Morphine as the drug of choice by addicts

The addictive qualities of Heroin were not understood for many decades after it's initial distribution.

January 1, 1955 the importation of Heroin was prohibited in Canada

The balance of Heroin entering Canada has its origins in the tri-border area of Southeast Asia.

This area is known as the "Golden Triangle".

The Golden Triangle consists of North Eastern Myanmar (formerly known as Burma), Northern Thailand, and Northern Laos

Colombia has also entered the market as a major importer of Heroin.

In the United States in 1998, 65% of the Heroin seized came from Colombia

More recently, the country of Afghanistan has become a major exporter of Heroin

Ice $C_{10}H_{15}N$

Key Facts

What is it?	Crystal Methamphetamine Central Nervous System Stimulant
Physiological Responses	Nervousness Sweating Sleeplessness Loss of Appetite
Eye Characteristics	Constricted or dilated, extremely rapid eye-movement
Rhomberg Internal Clock	Slow
How long do the effects last?	May last up to 16 hours
Onset of Action	The drug has a rapid onset of action which occurs within seconds
Effects of Use	The euphoria experienced is similar to base Cocaine, however the effects last much longer
How is it Taken?	ICE is normally smoked in a pipe, however it can be ground into a powder and injected or inhaled
Negative Effects of Use	Rapid heart and respiration rates Confusion Extreme Paranoia Strong violent tendencies Withdrawal from ICE causes severe depression

Heroin

Ice

Other Information Related to Ice

Possibility of Physical Addiction	Extremely addictive
Physical Characteristics of Substance	ICE appears as clear, shiny crystals, varying in size from the size of rice grains to the size of the last joint of your baby finger
Odours Associated to Substance	Chemical smell when burned
Drug Paraphernalia	Broken light bulbs which are used as pipes. Tin Foil
Dosage	ICE is measured in tenths of grams Each tenth of one gram equates to 3 to 4 "hits"
Safety Issues for Medical Personnel	Users can be extremely paranoid Extreme Violent Tendencies
Associated Drugs	Base Cocaine
Street Pricing	Tenth of a gram - $5 - $50 Gram - $40 - $100 Ounce - $3,600 - $7,000 One Kilo - $90,000 - $95,000
Common Street Names	Ice, Glass Crystal Ice Cream Batu Shabu
Other Dangers	Users can engage in binge type behaviour and go without sleep or food for days

To clarify the origins of this substance, it should be pointed out that Ice is Methamphetamine that has been converted from its original form via a very simple chemical process. A simple analogy that can be drawn would be to say that Ice is to Methamphetamine what Crack is to Cocaine.

NOTES

Ice

Inhalants

Key Facts

What is it?	Central Nervous System Depressant
Physiological Responses	Tiredness
	Nausea and vomiting
	Nosebleeds
	Exhilaration
	Slurred speech
	Drunken appearance
	Irritation of nose and eyes
	Chemical odour on breath and clothes
	Blank expression
	Lack of inhibitions
	Loss of appetite
Eye Characteristics	Near normal pupil size
	Irritation
	Near normal response of pupils to light stimulus
Rhomberg Internal Clock	Near normal
How long do the effects last?	Because intoxication lasts only a few minutes, abusers frequently seek to prolong the high by continuing to inhale repeatedly over the course of several hours
Onset of Action	Within minutes of inhalation
Effects of Use	After heavy use of inhalants, abusers may feel drowsy for several hours and experience a lingering headache
How is it Taken?	Sniffing or snorting fumes from a container

	Spraying aerosols directly into the nose or mouth
	"Bagging"-sniffing or inhaling fumes from substances sprayed or deposited inside a plastic or paper bag
	Huffing from an inhalant soaked rag stuffed in the mouth
	Inhaling from balloons filled with Nitrous Oxide
Negative Effects of Use	Liver and kidney damage
	Nerve damage
	Brain damage
	Heart beats erratically
	Hypoxia of the central nervous system
	Instant heart failure
	Throat, nasal and lung damage
	Teeth and gum damage
	Suffocation
	Coma
	Death

Other Information Related to Inhalants

Possibility of Physical Addiction	Compulsive use and a mild withdrawal syndrome can occur with long-term inhalant abuse
	A strong need to continue using inhalants
	With regular use, tolerance develops
Physical Characteristics of Substance	Variety of characteristics but include:
	Paint
	Solvents
	Aerosols
	Airplane glue
	Nail polish remover

Odours Associated to Substance	Variety, but tend to be chemical in nature
Drug Paraphernalia	Plastic bags
	Paper bags
	Balloons
	Rags
Dosage	N/A
Safety Issues for Medical Personnel	Belligerence
	Impaired Judgement
	Violence
	Loss of self control
	Losing touch with one's surroundings
Associated Drugs	Alcohol
	Tranquillizers
Street Pricing	This varies because of the use of household products such as aerosol non-stick cooking and disinfecting sprays.
	Gasoline
Common Street Names	Snappers
	Poppers
	Texas Shoe Shine
	Laughing Gas
Other Dangers	Sudden sniffing death syndrome
	Complications to reproductive organs
	Serious burn injuries

The problem with inhalants is not a new one but it has such adverse effects because of the nature of these drugs. One of the biggest issues is the age of the users. This particular form of drug appeals to the age group of 7 to 17 year olds.

Inhalants are a very difficult group of drugs to control because they are available under most kitchen sinks.

These drugs are known as vasodilators because when inhaled, they produce the sensation of heat and excitement by dilating the blood vessels.

Inhalants fall into four categories:

Aerosols: These are sprays that may contain propellants and solvents. They include vegetable oils, hair sprays and deodorants

Volatile Solvents: These are liquids that vaporize at room temperatures. They are found in common household products like paint thinners, gasoline, glues, corrections fluids and felt tip markers

Gases: These include medical anaesthetics like Ether, Chloroform, Nitrous Oxide, or "Laughing Gas". Household or commercial products containing gases include butane lighters, propane tanks, whipped cream dispensers, and refrigerants.

Nitrites: These particular inhalants dilate blood vessels and relax muscles. Nitrites include Cyclohexyl Nitrite, Isoamyl (amyl) Nitrite, and Isobutyl (butyl) Nitrite. Cyclohexyl nitrite is found in room deodorizers. Amyl Nitrite is used in certain diagnostic procedures and is prescribed to some patients for heart pain. Illegally diverted ampoules of Amyl Nitrite are called "Poppers" or "Snappers" on the street. Butyl Nitrite is an illegal substance that is often packaged and sold in small bottles also referred to as "Poppers."

L.S.D. Lysergic Acid Diethylamide $C_{20}H_{25}N_3O$

Key Facts

What is it?	Hallucinogen
Physiological Responses	Hypertension or hypo tension
	Tachycardia (rapid heart rate)
	Tachypnea (rapid breathing)
	Vomiting
	Diarrhoea
	Salivation
	Anorexia
	Acutely altered mental status, characterized by:
	• Restlessness
	• Acute anxiety
	• Behavioural changes
	• Depersonalization
	Tremors
	Incoordination
	Abnormally rapid and deep breathing
	High blood pressure
	Elevated body temperature
	Insomnia
	Nausea and vomiting
	Suppression of appetite
	Acute panic
	Bizarre behaviour
	Hallucinations
	Flashbacks
	Indications of LSD Exposure
	Altered cognitive and perceptual states
	Visual hallucinations
	Behavioural changes

	Paranoia
	Marked fluctuations in mood
	Acute psychotic reactions
	Dizziness
	Diaphoresis (sweating) may also occur
Eye Characteristics	Pupil dilation (Mydriasis)
	Lacrimation (tearing)
	Impaired perception of colour, and other visual functions
	Persistent or recurrent visual illusions
	Halos around objects
Rhomberg Internal Clock	Fast
How long do the effects last?	Effects last from 8-12 hours
Onset of Action	15 to 45 minute onset of action
Effects of Use	Appetite suppressant
	Hallucinogenic
	Altered sense of reality
	Heightened sense of spirituality
How is it Taken?	Most commonly, L.S.D. is ingested orally, however, it may be sniffed (inhaled) in powdered form or injected in solution (water soluble)
	L.S.D. is odourless, colourless, and tasteless
	The forms of this drug are:
	Tablet
	Capsule
	Sugar cubes
	Candies or other foodstuffs
	The most common form is blotter

L.S.D.

Negative Effects of Use	Vivid perceptual distortions
	Distortion of time and distance
	Recent or long forgotten memories resurface
	Insignificant thoughts take on deep meaning
	Overdose
	Death

Other Information Related to L.S.D.

Possibility of Physical Addiction	L.S.D. is not physically addictive however, the drug's potent mind altering effects can lead to chronic use
	The more a person uses L.S.D. the more they need to use.
	Complete tolerance depends on dosage and frequency of use however, all things being equal, complete tolerance is achieved after a person takes 3 to 4 daily doses
	Tolerance disappears after 4 to 5 days of non use
Physical Characteristics of Substance	Generally found on blotter paper in the form of cartoon or video characters
	Colourless
	Allegedly has a bitter taste
Odours Associated to Substance	Odourless
Drug Paraphernalia	Blotter papers that look like cartoon or video characters
Dosage	Normal dosage: 125- 200 micrograms
	Usual street dose: 30 to 300 micrograms

	Psychedelic dose: 100 to 750 micrograms
	Minimum effect dose: 25 micrograms
	Lethal dose: .2 to 1 milligram
Safety Issues for Medical Personnel	Extremely Violent
Associated Drugs	Ecstasy, Psilocybin
Street Pricing	2 hits - $5
Common Street Names	Acid
	Cid
	Blue
	Pink
	Window Pane
	Sunshine
	Orange Sunshine
	Blotter
	Microdots
	Paper
Other Dangers	Violent or hazardous behaviour
	Brain damage
	Accidental fatalities
	Homicides
	Self-mutilation
	Suicide
	Congenital abnormalities in offspring
	Deaths from L.S.D. are usually due to trauma that occurs during hallucinations.
	Stages of the L.S.D. "Trip"
	Stage I. (Somatic) 0-60 minutes; light-headedness, twitching, flushing, hypertension, dilation of pupils
	Stage II. (Perceptual) 30-60 minutes; visual and auditory sensory alterations,

distortions of colours, distortion of
distance, shape, and time

Stage III. (Psychic) 2-12 hours; euphoria,
mood swings, depression,
depersonalization, derealization, loss of
body image

L.S.D. a brief history;

Dr. Albert Hoffman first synthesized this drug in
Switzerland in 1938. It is produced in clandestine
laboratories and is derived from Lysergic Acid.
Lysergic Acid comes from the Ergot Fungus which
grows on the grain, rye. The drug can also be produced from Lysergic Acid Amide which is a
chemical found in the seeds of the Morning Glory
flower. This drug became very popular in the
1960's and has remained a popular drug of choice,
especially among young people. One of the major
reasons the drug is popular is the relatively low
cost.

Marihuana (Marijuana - U.S. spelling)

Key Facts

What is it?	Central Nervous System Depressant
Physiological Responses	Lowered heart rate Lowered respiration Appear drowsy Lethargic
Eye Characteristics	Pupil size is near normal, however, the pupil response to light is slow. THC causes the Sclera (white of the eye) to change to opaque red
Rhomberg Internal Clock	Distorted
How long do the effects last?	Effects last from 3 – 5 hours
Onset of Action	Within Seconds when smoked
Effects of Use	Euphoria associated to the production of Endorphin Relaxed Calm Appetite is stimulated Nausea is inhibited
How is it Taken?	Smoked in a cigarette called a joint or blunt or in a pipe Can be ingested
Negative Effects of Use	Causes mental confusion Inappropriate emotional response Sexual reproductive organs negatively affected Short term memory recall inhibited

L.S.D.

Marihuana

Distorts senses (sights and sounds are exaggerated)

Hand-eye coordination affected

Impairs motor skills

Stunts emotional and intellectual growth

Cannot judge speed, distance or time

Some users even have visual hallucinations

Other Information Related to Marihuana

Possibility of Physical Addiction	Addiction to T.H.C. is possible and a psychological dependence can also develop.
Physical Characteristics of Substance	Green plant, the bud or flower of the plant is the most sought after component
Odours Associated	The plant has a skunk like smell. When it is burnt there is a sweet, pungent smell.
Drug Paraphernalia	Pipes Cigarette papers Knives that are scorched on the ends (hot knifing)
Dosage	Approximately 80 marihuana cigarettes per ounce (.3 of 1 gram per cigarette)
Safety Issues for Medical Personnel	Causes panic attacks and paranoia – may feel threatened by authority figures
Associated Drugs	Alcohol
Street Pricing	1 joint - $5.00 $15 per gram or 2 grams for $25 1/8th ounce (3.5 grams) $40 $280 per ounce $2,800 to $3,300 per pound

Common Street Names	Weed
	Chronic
	Pot
	Grass
	Green
	Skunk
Other Dangers	Increased potency of T.H.C. causes users to have longer highs and greater levels of intoxication.
	Smoke from Marihuana cigarettes contains more toxins and carcinogens than the smoke generated by cigarette tobacco
	Humans store T.H.C. in the fat molecules.
	If enough T.H.C. is stored, eventually a dump of the substance is experienced and the user is subjected to a "flashback" high.

Marihuana

The most active ingredient in marihuana is a substance identified as Delta 9- Tetrahydro-cannabinol (T.H.C.). For the most part, this is what makes Cannabis Marihuana illegal and this substance is causing some controversy with respect to medicinal use. The T.H.C. content in most Marihuana available today has increased and this has had a direct impact on the potency of the Marihuana. A generation ago, the average T.H.C. content in Marihuana was approximately 1%. Today these averages in some regions are up over 17%. This increase has been achieved through some scientific methods (i.e. cloning and crossbreeding plant strains) and also through trial and error of individual growers. There are 3 varieties of the marihuana plant;

- Cannabis Sativa
- Cannabis Indica
- Cannabis Ruderalis

Through genetics and microchemistry and microbiology, the Marihuana today contains far higher levels of T.H.C. These high levels have altered the drug and affected the high that is experienced by consumers. The most common way to obtain T.H.C. from Marihuana is to smoke the Marihuana although some individuals obtain the T.H.C. by ingesting the Marihuana. As outlined in the key facts reference chart, (page 39) if you smoke Marihuana, you will begin to feel the effects within seconds. Due to the increased T.H.C. content, these effects last longer and are more profound in comparison to the effects of the Marihuana from a generation ago. A recent study that was conducted in the United States concluded that T.H.C. is actually physically addictive, and this substance reacts to our brain chemistry the same way the opiates (Opium, Morphine, Heroin) do. This is rather significant in so much as prior to this revelation, T.H.C. was thought to cause psychological dependence, but not physical addiction. A recent study conducted in British Columbia concluded that 48% of the 12-17 year olds who were being treated in provincial treatment centres for substance abuse were being treated for addiction to T.H.C. A popular derivative of Marihuana is the resin. This is usually seen in two forms; Marihuana Oil and Hashish. Both are by-products of the Marihuana plant and are potent forms of T.H.C. The oil is seen in a very thick paste, which is dark green in colour. Hashish is formed into very hard bricks and is sold in chunks. Both forms of the resin are normally smoked. At the street level, the oil is normally packaged in 1gram glass vials. Hashish at this level is normally packaged in 1gram cubes wrapped in tin foil. The pricing structure of the resin parallels the Marihuana's.

NOTES

Methamphetamine $C_{10}H_{15}N$

Key Facts

What is it?	Central Nervous System Stimulant
Physiological Responses	Increased Alertness
	Sense of Well-being
	Hallucinations
	Paranoia
	Intense High
	Aggressive Behaviour
	Convulsions
	Increased Heart rate
	Extreme Rise in Body Temperature
	Uncontrollable movements (twitching, jerking, etc)
	Violent Tendencies
	Insomnia
	Impaired Speech
	Dry, itchy skin
	Loss of Appetite
	Acne Sores
	Numbness
Eye Characteristics	Slow to react to light stimulus
	Dilated or constricted pupils
Rhomberg Internal Clock	Fast
How long do the effects last?	Effects of its use can last from 8 to 24 hours
	Oral ingestion or snorting produces a long lasting high instead of a rush, which reportedly can continue for as long as 12 hours.
Onset of Action	Snorting produces effects within 3 to 5 minutes, and oral ingestion

	produces effects within 15 to 20 minutes.
	Dose dependant but generally occurs within seconds to minutes
Effects of Use	Increased Alertness
	Sense of Well-being
	Hallucinations
	Intense High
	Loss of Appetite
How is it Taken?	Methamphetamine can be swallowed, injected or inhaled
	Pills (gelcaps, tablets)
	Powder
	Chunks
Negative Effects of Use	Fatal Kidney and Lung Disorders
	Brain Damage
	Depression
	Permanent Psychological Problems
	Violent and Aggressive Behaviour
	Weight Loss
	Behaviour resembling paranoid schizophrenia
	Malnutrition
	Disturbance of Personality Development
	Lowered Resistance to Illness
	Liver Damage
	Stroke
	Death
	Effects on the Mind
	Disturbed Sleep
	Excessive Excitation
	Excessive Talking
	Panic
	Anxiousness

Methamphetamine

	Nervousness
	Moodiness & Irritability
	False Sense of Confidence and Power
	Delusions of Grandeur Leading to Aggressive Behaviour
	Uninterested in Friends, Sex, or Food
	Severe Depression

Other Information Related to Methamphetamine

Possibility of Physical Addiction	Extremely addictive substance which produces a severe craving
Physical Characteristics of Substance	In its original form, it is a powder which can vary in colour
Odours Associated to Substance	The users have an unpleasant body odour
Drug Paraphernalia	Needles
Dosage	Normal dose; 25-50 mgs
Safety Issues for Medical Personnel	**Can be extremely violent** Six steps in dealing with a Tweaker: Keep your distance Lower the lights Slow your speech and lower your voice Slow your movements Keep your hands visible Keep the Tweaker talking
Associated Drugs	Alcohol, Heroin

Street Pricing	Generally purchased in 1gram quantities that cost $150. This drug is so powerful, that it is often purchased by the 10th of gram. At this level, this dose is referred to as a hit and sold for $40.00 per hit
	At the wholesale level, the cost is approximately $7,000 to $10,000 per pound
Common Street Names	Speed
	Crank
	Crystal
	Fast or "Go Fast"
	Quick
	Grit
Other Dangers	High intensity abusers and binge abusers of Methamphetamine enter into a seven stage abuse cycle
	This cycle takes weeks to complete
	First Stage of Abuse: RUSH
	This response is associated to smoking or injecting Methamphetamine
	It lasts from 5 to 30 minutes
	Body metabolism increases
	Heart rate, blood pressure and pulse soar
	Feelings of pleasure are experienced
	Second Stage of Abuse: HIGH
	During this stage the abuser feels aggressively smarter and may become argumentative
	The high stage can last between 4 to 16 hours

Methamphetamine

Third Stage of Abuse: **BINGE**

This stage consists of a 3 to 15 day high where the abuser continues to consume Methamphetamine

During this stage, with each ingestion of the drug a diminishing RUSH is achieved until finally there is no rush or high

During a binge, the abuser becomes mentally and physically hyperactive in attempting to maintain the HIGH as long as possible

Fourth Stage of Abuse: **TWEAKING**

This is the most dangerous stage of the cycle

At this stage nothing the abuser does can take away the emptiness the binge has created

This includes taking more Methamphetamine

Some "Tweakers" will take depressants such as Alcohol or Heroin to ease the feelings of emptiness experienced in this stage

Confronting a Tweaker can be a catalyst to violent behaviour

A Tweaker has likely been 3 to 15 days without sleep.

They will crave Methamphetamine and will have a strong feeling of uncontrollable frustration

A Tweaker's movements are brisk, their eyes are clear, however move ten times faster than normal

Tweakers exist in a world where hallucinations are vivid and they do not need provocation to react violently to situations

Tweakers have a tendency to arm themselves and participate in crimes of opportunity

Fifth Stage of Abuse: **CRASH**

During this stage, the abuser sleeps from 1 to 3 days revitalizing their body

Sixth Stage of Abuse: **NORMAL**

This stage lasts from 2 to 14 days.

During this time the abuser returns to a normal state which is slightly deteriorated from that prior to the BINGE stage

As the frequency of the binge increases, the duration and degree of "normal" decreases

Seventh Stage of Abuse: **WITHDRAWAL**

At this stage, the abusers realize they are withdrawing from the effects of the drug, and will therefore become depressed and suicidal

Ten to twenty percent of abusers who seek treatment for Methamphetamine dependence actually succeed in defeating this cycle of abuse

Methamphetamine is a synthetic Central Nervous System stimulant that is produced illegally in clandestine laboratories. Many of the laboratories that produce this substance are controlled by organized crime and there is a historic link between the production of this substance and the outlaw motorcycle gangs.

The prototype of Methamphetamine is the drug Amphetamine. Amphetamine was first synthesized in 1887 and is structurally related to the natural occurring stimulant Ephedrine. In the late 1960's Methamphetamine that was and still is commonly referred to, as "speed" became a popular drug of choice.

Methamphetamine is a highly addictive, very dangerous street drug. A recent study out of California concludes that if Methamphetamine is tried once there is a 42% chance of addiction, if Methamphetamine is tried more than once, there is a 96% chance of addiction. The success rate for the recovery of individuals who have been addicted to this drug is approximately 20%; this leaves 80% of the addicts untreatable and actively consuming the drug.

It is a powerful hallucinogenic Amphetamine that comes in many forms. These forms include; pill, gel cap, chunks, and powder. The drug can be consumed in different ways; it can be swallowed, inhaled, (snorted) injected, or smoked. In its original form it is soluble in water. Like Cocaine, there are several public safety issues surrounding the production, distribution and use of this drug.

Firstly due to its potency, the drug is, as mentioned, highly addictive and produces a severe craving. This combination leads the consumers of the drug down a dangerous path, as it is also very expensive. Once a habit has been developed, most users cannot afford to finance the use in a traditional manner and subsequently turn to street crime. An aggravating factor is the effects of use, which among other things leads the user to violent, paranoid behaviour. Other effects of use are:

- Increased alertness
- Euphoria
- Hallucinations
- Increase in all the metabolic rates

There are also very serious health ramifications associated to long-term use, these include; kidney and lung failure, heart disease and death. In our country, due to the social nature of our medical system, individuals who chronically abuse this drug not only contribute statistical data to our crime rate but also place a burden on our health care system.

This drug can be smoked. This form of the drug is referred to as "Ice" and is extremely potent and addictive. Whether in the original or smokeable form, the drug has a long-lasting life. Effects of one dose can last from 6 to 18 hours. This is another public safety issue as with the use of the drug, its users can be under the influence and very intoxicated for long periods of time. These periods of time are filled with violent and paranoid thoughts, hallucinations, and poor judgment and decision-making skills.

The next most significant public safety issue is how this drug is manufactured. As mentioned, the production of Methamphetamine is illegally done in clandestine laboratories. These labs are managed by individuals, who for the most part have not been professionally trained in the proper handling of chemicals or chemical reactions. The "cooks" who produce the drug are responsible for handling pre-cursor chemicals and reagents that are flammable, explosive, toxic and caustic. In an urban setting the danger to the public is amplified as many of these laboratories are discovered in the midst of highly populated communities. Simply put, these laboratories are inherently dangerous and pose a profound hazard to the public at large.

In summary, Methamphetamine regardless of which form it takes is a dangerous, highly addictive substance, which has a significant negative impact on our society. Law enforcement agencies across North America are becoming more and more involved with the interdiction of this drug. The major reason this is occurring is that organized criminals who care nothing for public safety, have discovered the relative ease with which this drug can be produced, and the profit that can be made by distributing it.

Psilocybin $C_{12}H_{17}N_2O_4P$

Key Facts

What is it?	Hallucinogen
Physiological Responses	Increased blood pressure and heart rate
	Nausea and vomiting
	Elevated body temperature
	Sweating
Eye Characteristics	Possible dilation, pupil response to light stimuli is near normal
Rhomberg Internal Clock	Slow
How long do the effects last?	3 to 6 hours
Onset of Action	Onset of action is 15 to 45 minutes
Effects of Use	Vivid perceptual distortions
	Users perceptions of their bodies may be distorted
	They may experience sensations of heaviness or feelings of floating
	Synesthesia frequently occurs (the user can "see" music or "hear" colours)
	All sensory experiences tend to be heightened
	The user perceives brighter colours, sharper definition of objects, increased hearing acuity, more sharply distinguished sense of taste
	Users often experience difficulties in concentrating and focusing their attention
	Memory is impaired and the users sense of the present reality may be temporarily lost
	Users may be intensely preoccupied with trivial thoughts and objects

Methamphetamine

Psilocybin

	Users may feel they are undergoing a profound mystical or spiritual experience
How is it Taken?	The mushroom itself may be eaten, either fresh or dried
	Psilocybin may also be inhaled, smoked, or injected
	Synthetic Psilocybin can be taken orally in tablets or capsules
	Psilocybin powder mixed with fruit juice "fungus delight" is a common form of preparation for oral ingestion
Negative Effects of Use	Panic
	Terror
	Paranoid Thinking
	Depression
	Severe Agitation
	Fearfulness
	Hazardous or Life Threatening Behaviour
	Nausea and Vomiting
	Abdominal Cramps

Other Information Related to Psilocybin

Possibility of Physical Addiction	A tolerance which is similar to the tolerance to L.S.D. develops rapidly, the user must periodically discontinue use to regain original sensitivity. There is little evidence of physical addiction.
Physical Characteristics of Substance	Dried brown mushrooms
	It is possible to produce synthetic Psilocybin. In this form, it appears as a white crystalline powder
Odours Associated to Substance	None

Drug Paraphernalia	None
Dosage	4 - 6 milligrams= minimum effect
	7 – 20 milligrams= moderate effect
	30 – 60 milligrams= full blown effect
	15 to 20 milligrams of Psilocybin produce the same effect as 100 micrograms of L.S.D.
	These milligram doses would be achieved by purchasing 1 to 5 grams of the bulk mushroom form
Safety Issues for Medical Personnel	Users can be paranoid and are subject to irrational thinking, they may also engage in hazardous behaviour which may prove dangerous to first responders
Associated Drugs	L.S.D. and Mescaline
Street Pricing	1 gram - $8.00
	1 ounce - $50.00 to $100.00
	1 pound - $600.00 to $1,000.00
Common Street Names	Magic Mushrooms, Coppertops
	Shrooms, Mush, Pixie Dust, Pot Dust
Other Dangers	A cross tolerance to the associated drugs (L.S.D. and Mescaline) may develop

Psilocybin

SYMPTOM CHART

SYMPTOM	POSSIBLE DRUGS
Acne Sores	METHAMPHETAMINE
Aggressive Behaviour	METHAMPHETAMINE
Alertness	METHAMPHETAMINE
Anorexia	LSD, ECSTASY
Anxiety	ECSTASY, LSD, METHAMPHETAMINE
Appetite Stimulated	MARIHUANA
Appetite Suppression	LSD, METHAMPHETAMINE, ECSTASY
Blurred vision	ECSTASY
Calm	MARIHUANA
Confusion	ICE, COCAINE, MARIHUANA
Constipation	HEROIN
Convulsions	ECSTASY, METHAMPHETAMINE
Dehydration	ECSTASY
Delusions of grandeur	METHAMPHETAMINE
Deperson-alization	LSD
Depression	METHAMPHETAMINE, ICE, ECSTASY
Diaphoresis	LSD
Diarrhoea	LSD
Dizziness	LSD
Difficulty Concentrating	ECSTASY, PSILOCYBIN
Drowsiness	HEROIN, MARIHUANA
Dry, Itchy Skin	METHAMPHETAMINE
Euphoria	MARIHUANA
Excitation	METHAMPHETAMINE

Eye movement rapid	ICE
False sense of confidence	METHAMPHETAMINE
False sense of power	METHAMPHETAMINE
Flashbacks	LSD, MARIHUANA
Hallucinations	ECSTASY, LSD, METHAMPHETAMINE, PSILOCYBIN
Heart rate increased	METHAMPHETAMINE, ICE
Heart rate reduced	HEROIN, MARIHUANA
Hypertension	LSD, ECSTASY
Hypotension	LSD, HEROIN, MARIHUANA
Impaired Speech	METHAMPHETAMINE
Incoordination	LSD, MARIHUANA
Increased body temperature	ECSTASY, METHAMPHETAMINE, COCAINE
Increased pulse rate	ECSTASY
Intense High	METHAMPHETAMINE, BASE COCAINE
Insomnia	ECSTASY, LSD, METHAMPHETAMINE
Irrational behaviour	ECSTASY
Irritability	METHAMPHETAMINE, MARIHUANA (withdrawal symptom)
Jaw clenching	ECSTASY
Lacrimation	LSD
Lethargy	MARIHUANA

Symptoms

Malnutrition	HEROIN, METHAMPHETAMINE, COCAINE
Moodiness	LSD, METHAMPHETAMINE
Mydriasis	LSD, METHAMPHETAMINE, ICE
Nausea	ECSTASY, HEROIN, LSD
Nausea Inhibited	MARIHUANA
Nervousness	METHAMPHETAMINE, ICE
Numbness	METHAMPHETAMINE
Panic	LSD, METHAMPHETAMINE, ICE
Paranoia	ECSTASY, LSD, METHAMPHETAMINE
Psychotic Reactions	LSD
Relaxed	MARIHUANA
Respiration Decreased	GHB, HEROIN, MARIHUANA
Respiration Increased	COCAINE, ECSTASY, ICE, METHAMPHETAMINE
Restlessness	LSD
Salivation	LSD
Sclera turns opaque red	MARIHUANA
Sensations of floating	ECSTASY
Short term memory inhibited	MARIHUANA
Sleeplessness	METHAMPHETAMINE, ICE
Slow gait	HEROIN
Slowed slurred speech	HEROIN
Sweating	ECSTASY, ICE
Teeth grinding	ECSTASY

Tachycardia	LSD
Tachypnea	LSD
Talking excessively	COCAINE, ECSTASY, METHAMPHETAMINE
Tremors	LSD, METHAMPHETAMINE
Violent Tendencies	METHAMPHETAMINE, ICE, COCAINE
Visual Illusions	LSD, ECSTASY, METHAMPHETAMINE
Vomiting	HEROIN, LSD

NOTES

Glossary of Terms

A	Amphetamines
A BOMB	Mixture of Marihuana and Heroin
ACID	L.S.D. (Lysergic Acid Diethylamide)
ACID HEAD	L.S.D. user
ADAM	Ecstasy (Methalenedioxymeth-amphetamine) Central Nervous System Stimulant Hallucinogenic Amphetamine
AMPED	To be under the influence or addicted to Methamphetamine
AMPHETAMINE	A central nervous system stimulant synthetically produced
ANGEL DUST	Phencyclidine
AROUND THE TURN	Going through withdrawal
ARTILLERY	Equipment for injecting drugs
BACK-UP	Permitting blood back into a syringe to ensure penetration of a vein
BACKTRACK	To withdraw the plunger within the syringe after the needle is inserted into the vein, if the action draws blood into the syringe, then the needle is properly inserted and there is no air present
BAD TRIP	Feeling of fear with depression arising in some cases following use of drugs
BAG	A quantity of drugs or a mood, direction style or taste
BANG	To inject drugs, a rush – an intense orgasmic–like sensation
BAR	Solid brick of Marihuana

BARBS	Barbiturates
BATU	Crystal Methamphetamine (Ice)
BAYONET	Hypodermic syringe
BENNIES	Benzedrine and Amphetamines
BINDLE	A deck (Quantity of Drug)
BINGE	Refers to a sustained period of drug use
BLASTED	Be under the influence of drugs
BLOTTER	L.S.D.
BLOW	Cocaine
BLOW HORSE	Sniff (snort) Heroin
BLUE	L.S.D.
BOOTING	Snorting Cocaine
BOMBITA	Heroin and Cocaine combined
BREAD	Money
BRICK	Kilo of Marihuana, Opium, Morphine in a compressed brick form
BRING IT UP	To dilate a vein prior to injection
BUD	Marihuana
BULBING	Using household light bulbs as methamphetamine pipes
BUMMER	A bad trip or unpleasant experience
BUNDLE	25 capsules of heroin
BURNED	To receive phoney narcotics or other drugs
BURNED OUT	A state of chronic behavioural impairment resulting from heavy drug use
BUSTED	Arrested
BUTTONS	The sections of the Peyote cactus or Peyote buttons
BUY	A purchase
BUZZ	A early high on a drug
CANDY	Cocaine
CANNABIS	The genus name for all the Tetrahydrocannibinol (THC) producing plants

CAP	Capsule containing drugs in granule, crystal, liquid or powdered form
CAVIAR	Residue from burned base cocaine
CHANNEL	Vein used for injecting drugs
CHASING THE DRAGON	Heroin placed on tin foil then heated from below and smoked
CHERRY METH	G.H.B. - Gamma-hydroxybutyrate
CHIPPING	Taking small amounts of drugs on an irregular basis
CID	L.S.D.
COKE	Cocaine
COLD TURKEY	Abrupt withdrawal without medication; the skin surface resembles the texture of a cold, plucked turkey
COMING DOWN	Recovery from a drug experience, losing the effects of the drug
CONNECTION	The source of the illegal drugs, the pusher or middle man
COOK	Dissolving powdered narcotics in preparation for injection by mixing with water and heating the solution in a spoon over the flame
COPPER TOP	Psilocybin
COTTON SHOT	Water added to saturated cotton to remove the remaining heroin.
CRANK	Methamphetamine
CRYSTAL	The crystalline form of speed or Methamphetamine
DEALER	Drug supplier
DECK	A container for holding drugs, usually a folded flap of paper
DEPRESSANT	A drug which decreases the rate of bodily activity
DEXIES	Dexedrine, an Amphetamine, the midnight runners
DIME BAG	Ten dollars worth of drugs, usually Cannabis

DOWN	Heroin
DOWNERS	Sedatives, barbiturates, tranquillizers, alcohol and narcotics
DROP	To ingest a pill or capsule orally
DUST	A drug in powdered form
DUSTING	Combining Marihuana and Heroin, commonly known as "coco-puffs"
E'S	Ecstasy
ECKIES	Ecstasy
EIGHTHS	A measure of drug by weight as a fraction of an ounce. In cocaine deals, it's called an "eightball"
EVERCLEAR	G.H.B. - Gamma-hydroxybutyrate
EVERYTHING DRUG	Ecstasy
EYE OPENER	The first narcotic injection of the day
FACTORY	Clandestine laboratory or the equipment used for injecting drugs
FANTASY	G.H.B. - Gamma-hydroxybutyrate
FAST	Methamphetamine
FATTY	A Cannabis Marihuana joint
FIT	Paraphernalia for injecting drugs
FIX	To inject drugs
FLAKE	Cocaine
FLASHING	Inhaling glue or other solvents
FLASHBACK	A recurrence of a drug experience (usually LSD) without an additional dose of the drug
FREAKOUT	Lose touch with reality and have a bad experience
FRONT	To pay in advance of drug delivery or receipt of drugs before drug payment
G	G.H.B. - Gamma-hydroxybutyrate
GAMMA OH	G.H.B. - Gamma-hydroxybutyrate
GANJA	Marihuana

GBH	G.H.B. - Gamma-hydroxybutyrate
GHB	G.H.B. - Gamma-hydroxybutyrate
GEORGIA HOME BOY	G.H.B. - Gamma-hydroxybutyrate
GLASS	Ice
GO IN SEWER	Inject into vein
GOING DOWN	A happening, going on
GOOFBALL	Barbiturates, barbs, sleepers, downers
GRASS	Marihuana
GREAT HORMONES AT BEDTIME	G.H.B. - Gamma-hydroxybutyrate
GREEN	Marihuana
GRIEVOUS BODILY HARM	G.H.B.- Gamma-hydroxybutyrate
G-RIFFICK	G.H.B.- Gamma-hydroxybutyrate
GUN	Hypodermic needle and syringe
H	Heroin
H & C (speedball)	Mixture of Heroin and Cocaine
HABIT	The state of physical dependence
HARD	Crack Cocaine
HARD STUFF	Narcotic drugs; Heroin
HASH	Resin from the Cannibis Indica plant which contains a high THC content (Hashish)
HEAD	A heavy regular user of a drug, a person dependent on drugs
HEARTS	Heart shaped Dexedrine tablets
HEAT	A gun or the police
HIGH	Drug induced euphoria
HIT	Injection of drugs
HOG	Phencyclidine (PCP) also Angel Dust
HOOKAH	A pipe of Turkish origin used for smoking marihuana

HOOPING	Anal insertion of M.D.M.A.
HOOT	To smoke marihuana
HORSE	Heroin
HOT CAP	Unusually pure dose of Heroin
HOT LOAD	Overdose; lethal drug dose; usually refers to drugs deliberately given to eliminate a troublesome customer (pure Heroin, or Heroin mixture containing a poison such as Strychnine or Cyanide)
HUG DRUG	Ecstasy
HYPE	Addict
HYPO	Hypodermic needle
ICE	Crystal Methamphetamine
ICE CREAM	Crystal Methamphetamine
J OR JOINT	Marihuana cigarette
JACK UP	Inject slowly to prolong the effect of a drug or to be questioned by the police
JIB	G.H.B. - Gamma-hydroxybutyrate
JONESING	Needing or wanting drugs
JOY POP	Occasional injecting of narcotics (usually under the skin rather than in a vein)
JUNK	Heroin
JUNKIE	Heroin addict
K, KEE, KEY, KILO	One kilogram 2.2 lbs
KIF	Marihuana
KIT	Equipment for injecting drugs
LACE	Add one drug to another in order to produce a different or more potent effect
LEAF	Marihuana
LID	A quantity of Marihuana, usually one ounce
LINE	A unit dose of Cocaine, approximately 1/30 gram

LINES	Discolouration and scars, resulting from chronic injection
LIQUID E	G.H.B. - Gamma-hydroxybutyrate
LIQUID ECSTASY	G.H.B. - Gamma-hydroxybutyrate
LIQUID X	G.H.B. - Gamma-hydroxybutyrate
LOCO WEED	Marihuana
LOVE DRUG	Ecstasy
LSD	Lysergic Acid Diethylamide
LUDES	Quaalude, (powerful sedative drug)
M	Morphine
MAGIC MUSHROOM	Psilocybin
MAINLINE	To inject intravenously (shoot up)
MANICURE	To clean Cannabis of its stems and leaves
MARIHUANA	The flowering tops of the female plant which contains the majority of the THC content. (Bud)
MARY JANE	Marihuana
MDA	Methelenedioxyamphetamine, an hallucinogen
MESC	Mescaline, the alkaloid derivative of the Peyote Cactus
METH	Methamphetamine, or speed, a synthetic stimulant
METHADONE	Synthetic narcotic, Dolophine
MORNING GLORY	An hallucinogen with effects similar to LSD
MICRODOTS	L.S.D.
MUNCHIES	Hunger and constant snacking
MUSH	Psilocybin
MUSHROOMS	Psilocybin
NARC	Narcotic law enforcement officer
NEEDLE FREAK	Individuals who achieve gratification from the act of injecting

NICKEL BAG	A five dollar quantity of Cannabis - makes between five and eight joints
O.D.	Overdose
ON THE NOD	The sleep and relaxation after a shot of heroin
ORANGE SUNSHINE	L.S.D.
ORGANIC QUAALUDE	G.H.B. - Gamma-hydroxybutyrate
OUTFIT	Paraphernalia / equipment for injecting drugs
PAPER	L.S.D.
PARANOIA	A state of excited fear or anxiety that one is being persecuted or pursued
PCP	Phencyclidine
PEP PILLS	Amphetamines
PINK	L.S.D.
PIXIE DUST	Psilocybin
POP	To take a tablet or capsule orally or To inject just under the skin
POT	Marihuana
POT DUST	Psilocybin
POTENTIATION	The effect of two drugs taken together which is often more potent than taking either or both alone
POWDER	Cocaine
PSILOCYBIN	The alkaloid of certain hallucinogenic mushrooms
PSYCHEDELIC	Mind-altering, mind-manifesting
PSYCHOSIS	A general term for any major mental disorder associated with loss of contact with reality, often includes delusions, hallucinations or illusions
PSYCHO-TROPIC DRUGS	Drugs which alter or change the mental outlook, or other behavioural sensation

PUSHER	Supplier/ seller of drugs at the street level
QUICK	Methamphetamine
RAIL	A line of Cocaine
RAP	To discuss, talk at length
REEFER	Marihuana cigarette
RIG	A syringe
RIPPED	Highly intoxicated on drugs or Exhausted after extensive drug use or Adversely affected by a drug
RIPPED OFF	Cheated in a drug buy
ROACH	The butt-end of a Marihuana cigarette, which contains a high THC content that accumulates as the cigarette is burned
ROACH HOLDER/CLIP	A device that enables the smoker to hold a joint so it can be consumed to the very end without burning his or her fingers.
RUN	Any limited, but intense period of drug usage
RUSH	The intense orgasm-like euphoria experienced after injecting drugs
SALTY WATER	G.H.B. - Gamma-hydroxybutyrate
SCAG	Heroin
SCOOP	G.H.B. - Gamma-hydroxybutyrate
SCORE	To succeed in making a drug purchase
SCRATCH	Money
SET UP	A situation in which undercover police officers entice a person to sell drugs
SEWER	Vein
SHABU	Crystal Methamphetamine (Ice)
SHNAY	Cocaine
SHOOT UP	To inject with drugs intravenously
SHOOTING GALLERY	A place where Heroin addicts congregate to inject
SHROOMS	Psilocybin
SKIN POP	To inject under the skin

SMACK	Heroin
SNAPPERS	Inhalants
SNORT	To take Cocaine by inhaling it through the nose
SNOW	Cocaine
SNOW BIRD	Person dependent on Cocaine
SOAP	G.H.B. - Gamma-hydroxybutyrate
SOFT	Cocaine
SPEED	Methamphetamine
SPEED BALL	An injection which contains a stimulant and a depressant, often Cocaine mixed with Heroin
SPEED FREAK	Habitual user of speed
SPIKE	Hypodermic needle used for injecting drugs
SPLIFF	A Cannabis Marihuana joint, or oil on a cigarette paper
STASH	A place where drugs are hidden to prevent detection and seizure
STEP ON	To dilute a drug
STONED	The experience of being under the influence of drugs
STRAIGHT	A person who does not or who no longer uses drugs
STRUNG OUT	The emaciated and poor state of health and appearance due to chronic drug use
SUNSHINE	L.S.D.
SUPER GRASS	PCP sprinkled on marihuana
TABS	Tablets of capsules containing LSD
TANGING	Urine mixed with orange drink flavour crystals
TEXAS SHOE SHINE	Inhalants

THC	Tetrahydrocannabinol – identified as the group of substances which are responsible for the psychotoxicity and other pharmacological effects that accrue from the use of Cannabis
TIE UP	Apply a tourniquet to the arm or leg to produce distension of the vein
TOKE	A puff of a Marihuana cigarette
TOOT	Cocaine
TOTALLED	Exhausted after and acute drug experience
TRACKS/SNAKE	Marks and scars along the vein from repeated intravenous injections
TRANKS	Minor tranquillisers, downers
TRIP	The hallucinogenic experience following use of drugs, especially LSD
TURN ON	Introduce someone to a drug or to drugs
TWEAKING	Stage in Methamphetamine abuse cycle
UP	Cocaine
UP FRONT	A small quantity of drugs supplied to the buyer to indicate its quality or Showing the seller money before the drugs are produced
UPPERS	General term used for most stimulant drugs – Amphetamines, Cocaine, and psychedelic drugs
UP TIGHT	Tense, Nervous
USER	One who regularly takes drugs
WASTED	Exhausted after an acute drug experience or having a very bad drug experience or murdered
WATER	G.H.B. - Gamma-hydroxybutyrate
WEED	Marihuana
WEEKEND HABIT	Chipping
WIPED OUT	Exhausted after an acute drug experience
WHITE	Cocaine

WINDOW PANE	L.S.D.
WORKS	Paraphernalia/equipment for injecting drugs
WRECKED	Exhausted after an acute drug experience
X	Ecstasy
XTC	Ecstasy
YELLOW JACKETS	The colour of capsules
ZIG ZAG	Roll-your-own cigarette papers (often used for rolling joints)
ZOOMING	Being high on mushrooms
ZONKED	Extremely high on drugs

Bibliography

Marnell, Tim (ed) Drug Identification Bible 2nd Edition, Drug Identification Bible, Denver Colorado, 1995

Balster, R.L. Neural basis of inhalant abuse. Drug and Alcohol Dependence 51(1-2):207-214, 1998.

Bowen, S.E.; Wiley, J.L.; Evans, E.B.; Tokarz, M.E.; and Balster, R.L. Functional observational battery comparing effects of ethanol, 1,1,1-trichlorethane, ether, and flurothyl. Neurotoxicology and Teratology 18(5):577-585, 1996.

Brands, B; Sproule, B; Marshman, J. (eds) Drug and Drug Abuse, A Reference Text 3rd Edition, Government of Ontario Addiction Research Foundation, 1998

Domestic Marihuana Indoor Cultivation Operations; National Drug Intelligence Centre

Edwards, R.W., and Oetting, E.R. Inhalant use in the United States. In: Kozel, N.; Sloboda, Z.; and De La Rosa, M. (eds.), Epidemiology of Inhalant Abuse: An International Perspective. National Institute on Drug Abuse Research Monograph 148. DHHS Publication No. NIH 95-3831. Washington, DC: U.S. Government Printing Office, 8-28, 1995.

Fendrich, M.; Mackesy-Amiti, M.E.; Wislar, J.S.; and Goldstein, P.J. Childhood abuse and the use of inhalants: Differences by degree of use. American Journal of Public Health 87(5):765-769, 1997.

Jones, H.E., and Balster, R.L. Inhalant abuse in pregnancy. Obstetrics and Gynecology Clinics of North America 25(1): 153-167, 1997.

Marnell, Tim (ed) Drug Identification Bible 2nd Edition, pp 423 – 453; 319, 320, 1995

National Institute on Drug Abuse. National Survey Results on Drug Use From the Monitoring the Future Study, 1999 (www.monitoringthefuture.org).

National Institute on Drug Abuse. NIDA Infofax, Inhalants, 1999.

Riegel, A.C., and French, E.D. Acute toluene induces biphasic changes in rat spontaneous locomotor activity which are blocked by remoxipride. Pharmacology, Biochemistry and Behavior 62(3):399-402, 1999.

Rosenthal, E., The Marijuana Growers Guide, 1978

Sharp, C.W., and Rosenberg, N.L. Inhalants. In: Lowinson, J.H.; Ruiz, P.; Millman, R.B.; and Langrod, J.G. (eds.), Substance Abuse: A Comprehensive Textbook, 3d. ed. Baltimore: Williams and Wilkins, 246-264, 1996.

Sharp, C.W., and Rosenberg, N. Inhalant-related disorders. In: Tasman, A.; Kay, J.; and Lieberman, J.A. (eds.), Psychiatry, Vol. 1. Philadelphia: W.B. Saunders, 835-852, 1997.

Substance Abuse and Mental Health Services Administration. Population Estimates From the 1998 National Household Survey on Drug Abuse. SAMHSA, 1999.

Substance Abuse and Mental Health Services Administration. Summary Findings From the 1998 National Household Survey on Drug Abuse. SAMHSA, 1999.

Soderberg, L.S. Immunomodulation by nitrite inhalants may predispose abusers to AIDS and Karposi's Sarcoma. Journal of Neuroimmunology 83(1-2):157-161, 1998.

Soderberg, L.S. Increased tumor growth in mice exposed to inhaled isobutyl nitrite. Toxicology Letters 101(1-2):35-41, 1999.

Walton, S.C. Ecstasy: New Drug of Choice, Police Marksman Magazine, 2001

Walton, S.C. Clandestine Laboratory Investigation, Blue Line Magazine, 2000

Wesley, T. The Red Oil Report; A Documentary on the Activities of a Cannabis Oil Laboratory, 1980

Woody, G.F.; Donnell, D,; Seage, G.R.; et al. Non-injection substance use correlates with risky sex among men having sex with men: Data from HIV/NET. Drug and Alcohol Dependence 53(3).197-205, 1999.279(6): 22-26, 1998.

A Cognitive-Behavioral Approach: Treating Cocaine Addiction (1998) Manual 1 · NCADI # BKD254

A Collection of NIDA Notes Articles on Drug Abuse Prevention Research and the Community (1996) NCADI # NN0015

A Collection of NIDA Notes Articles on Drug Abuse Treatment (1998) NCADI # NN0026

NOTES

NOTES

Detective Steve Walton is available to lecture to groups anywhere with respect to the true perils of street drugs in our society today. If you or your organization is interested, please request a resume and lecture outline. E-mail us at dopeondope@shaw.ca or call us at 403-255-5605, toll free 877-255-1166 or fax 403-258-3696.

NOTES

NOTES

Get the Dope on Dope
A First Response Guide to Street Drugs
Order Form

Quantity	Description of Item	Price per Unit	Total Price
	First Response Guide to Street Drugs Volume I	$24.00	
	First Response Guide to Street Drugs Volume II	$28.00	
	11" x 17" Poster with Colour Photographs of the 10 street drugs in Volume I	$3.00	
		Total	

Shipping & Handling For Canada & USA:
1 Book: $6.00
Each additional book is $3.00 up to 25 books.
For orders larger than 25, please call
877-255-1166 for a customized quote
Prices do not include GST

For quantity orders, contact us at: Email: dopeondope@shaw.ca

Please Make Payment To Burnand Holding Co. Ltd.
420 52 Ave. S.W.
Calgary Alberta, Canada
T2V 0A9

Visa ❏   American Express ❏   Purchase Order ❏   Cert. Cheque ❏   Money Order ❏

Card # /Purchase Order # _____

Exp. Date _____ Name (as appears on card)_____

Cardholder's Signature _____

Your Address

Name: _____ E-mail Address: _____

Address: _____

City/Town: _____ Province/State: _____

Postal/Zip Code: _____ Country: _____

Work: (_____)_____ Home: (_____)_____

Cellular: (_____)_____ Fax: (_____)_____

This order form will have the same force and effect if received without original signature. Please allow up to 3 weeks for shipping.

Visit our Website at www.dopeondope.com or call us at 403-255-5605, email dopeondope@shaw.ca

Toll-Free 877-255-1166 or fax us at 403-258-3696.